Want More

A True Story of How Wanting Reveals a Way

By Schlitta Archibald-Patton

MAWMedia Group
Reno, NV

Publisher: MAWMedia Group

First Edition: October 2019

   Want More: A True Story of How Wanting Reveals a Way
/ By Schlitta Archibald-Patton

ISBN: 978-1-943616-21-3
MAWMedia Group, LLC
3095 Fairwood Dr
Reno, NV 89502
www.mawmedia.com

Dedications

To my daughter Tiara. I hope this book inspires and encourages you to follow your dreams. You have shared with me some great plans that you have which include big dreams that I can see coming to pass. Never give up on them and never let the fear you have about them win. Remember to be YOU! It's simple! Be the leader and never follow the crowd. I am so proud of the woman you have become. I can't wait to see all that GOD has planned for your life. You have an amazing spirit of courage, strength, ambition, and gratitude. I love you to infinity and I am so proud to call you my daughter!

To my baby girl Tamia Yvonne. I am so proud of you! You never give up! You go for what you want and if you get hurt about something, you address it and move forward with a different approach. You truly amaze me because I did not have the strength you have when I was your age. You handle hurdles and barriers by jumping right over them. For that, I am so grateful to GOD. I am always there to protect you, but you say "I got it momma. I'm ok." You are the caretaker for the whole family, even when it's not your position to do so. Always be Tamia. You will thrive and succeed (exceed!) in all you put your mind to do. Stay the course. Keep GOD first. And all will fall in place just as planned. I love you baby girl!

To my Husband Terence. You have seen my very low and my ugliest parts. Yet you have loved me the same. You have supported me and been there for me when I felt like I had no one to turn to. You have been my encouragement, support, and strength when I didn't have any left in me. You have also been my hype man. Thank you for your consistency! You have truly exemplified what it means to be a committed husband and a great father to our girls. I am so grateful to

GOD that he sent you 28 years ago into my life. From that day forward, you were all in! I love you Mr. Patton, and I can't wait to see all that GOD has planned for our family!

To my momma Patricia. You have been my strength during some of the most difficult times of my life. You are the strongest woman I know. As a child, I watched you make miracles happen and I have always wondered how you did it. When I got older and life happened, I remembered a lot of what you told me and shared with me about life and being the woman, I needed to be in this life. When I was younger, I didn't understand it all but, as I became an adult, I thanked GOD for a mother like you who never sugar coated a thing! Thank you, momma, for all the life lessons! I love you!

To my father Alton. Thank you, daddy, for always making a way. As a child, you taught and showed me how I was to be treated by a man. Your hard work and dedication to our family set every example of how my husband was to be. Nothing less! I love you daddy!

To my great aunt Martha who set a fine example of a true DIVA! Her honesty is what I will never forget. Our talks about life and how women were to be treated is what I will forever hold dear. I'm grateful to have had the time GOD allowed us to spend together and thankful for her confirmation that Terence would be my husband one day, something she'd always said since high school. I love and miss her dearly.

To "Nanny" Mattie Sue Patton. I am forever grateful for her. Our long talks about everything you could imagine, but most importantly, what she saw in me at a very young age. She helped Terence and I along the way of life to gain our independence and start a life of our own. I still remember her blunt words as she told Terence and I exactly what we needed to know, not always what we wanted to hear. I love and miss her dearly.

To Evelyn Yeargin. I affectionately call you "auntie." Thank you for the encouragement and for seeing more in Terence and me than we saw in ourselves. You helped break this fear I had of not being smart enough for college. You pushed me to a level beyond my own vision. You painted a picture I could not see coming to pass. Thank you for your continued support of our girls and our family. I love you for life!

To Dr. Michael Wright. Some people GOD truly brings into your life for a reason. You are one of them! My time at Tennessee State University was challenging but I held on. When I got the chance to take a course from you, my perspective and love for Social Work changed. I loved my social work courses, but your class was different. You showed so much interest in student's work, took the time to break down all that was needed to become a successful social worker, and even stayed after class to make sure we had it. You mentored me to a place where I was comfortable with my own work and theories. Thank you, Dr. Wright, for your mentoring and encouraging me to write this book while helping me overcome some of my fears. I am forever grateful for your mentorship and your friendship!

Contents

Prologue

I want to encourage you to follow your dreams. The fear will be there. That is just a sign to remind you that you are on a path toward something beyond the struggle, something more. Step out on fear when you don't have the faith. The fear does not have to rule. The faith will come.

I wish resilience for you. Overcome the challenges of life and awaken to the ability to thrive. Life requires work, but it is not all struggle. Take your time. Make consistent progress. Regret nothing.

Life. My parents struggled so much. They often talked about the life beyond the struggle—that there was more to life than struggle. I wanted more. I was fearful.

Courage. I couldn't allow the fear to stop me from getting more. I wanted to make my parents proud. I wanted to honor them by moving forward. They made progress. I built on that progress. My children will progress even farther. Along the way, I had to let go of the fear that was keeping me from having what I wanted out of life. The greatest was the fear of failure. I knew instinctively that my choices in the now impact my outcomes later in life. That knowledge allowed me to put the fear behind me. I moved forward because the good and the bad choices were mine to make. That ownership allowed me to follow my dreams.

Legacy. I wanted to develop a family of my own. I married a hard-working man who I honor by being the best wife I can be. I birthed two daughters who look up to me as their female role model. I want them to rise above their fear, access their resources, and do more than they thought was possible.

I want to support others, especially women, into Self-Knowledge, Purpose, Connection, and Building with other women. I want to support their healing through whatever their struggle or trauma was. Past tense because this moment forward can be more. I want to help them tell their success stories about how they overcame their fear, their greatest challenge, or the quest to find their purpose. I want to support women to benefit from courage beyond fear, life beyond struggle, and legacy beyond self just the way that I have. Some say, "College ain't for everybody." But it sure was for me!

Section I: The Foundation

Chapter 1: Wanting a Legacy

My mother didn't talk a lot about college. She was strict about graduating from high school because she hadn't. "Don't depend on anybody. Don't depend on any man." My mother never sugar coated anything in conversation. I felt comfortable talking with her about many things. Well, most everything. She was still my mother. So, she didn't hear about everything from me. She would tell you what you needed to hear not what you wanted to hear. I would complain about her bluntness sometimes, but she was always willing to explain what she was saying. Whatever the lecture, she was always careful to express that she had faith in me.

My dad was protective to a fault. He was strict because what he endured as a child. My mom often had to soften his restrictions. My dad had a difficult life. His father was killed just as he entered adulthood. He wasn't the oldest, but my father was tasked to help the family make ends meet and look out for his younger siblings. His mother was diagnosed with breast cancer and died when he was 15. She was sick for a long time. She died just as my mom and dad gave birth to my older sister. Today, if I would ask him about his childhood. He will switch to a totally different subject. Too difficult to discuss, I guess. All I know is that it was traumatic. He continues to be protective. If something happens with any of us, he wants to be notified. He has always been specific about how men were to treat me and respect him.

My father completed an 9th grade education. My mom hadn't completed much more. They instilled that there was opportunity for us to be educated beyond what they had achieved. They were adamant that my sisters and I complete high school. That was the goal. They had not completed, so they would ensure that we did. Together, my mother and father cleaned offices for a living. My mom wanted more for my sisters and me.

"We lucked up on jobs. Your granny lucked up on that government job after doing domestic work for many years. When you get older, you are not going to have any good government jobs without your high school diploma." My granny did get her GED later after she could no longer get a good job. My mother didn't want us to rely on luck. In her mind, this meant completing high school.

Discussing the System

For me, the major challenge was that I received no education about how the system works. I understood that I needed to finish high school. I knew that you need to do the work to make the grade. At least that was how it worked in high school. I felt like college was a different animal. I just didn't know the specifics. It just wasn't talked about. In my family, people didn't graduate, or they graduated high school and immediately got a job. In my family up until my generation, that's just what you do.

A great deal of the experience in my family focuses on survival. "A working man's hands" or "An honest living" is the goal for everyone. It seems to me that everyone recognizes the limitations and the costs of the pattern, but they seem unsure about ways to change their reality. My granny often complains about how her knees got bad, "Cleaning people's floors." I wanted to do something else that would not be so damaging to my knees. But I didn't know what that could be. "I want you to do better than me," my mom would always say. I kept that phrase. I repeat it to my daughter in just the same way. Yet now I know what better could be. I know that a process exists to get to better.

I ask my younger cousins now, "Where are you going to college?" I feel like I have said something that I shouldn't. The concept of college is not in their daily discussions. That was how it was with me growing up. Landing a "good job" was the goal. I had my heart set on the best option in the world of work. I wanted an office job. I thought that those people must make real money. They dress nice. They do things on the weekends. They go on vacations each Summer. I thought office work was a ticket to financial security and a lifestyle I could be proud of.

College Possibility

I struggled in school mainly due to an anxiety about my performance. I didn't feel that I could achieve more. I was not an A or B student. I C'd my way out of many classes. The idea developed in my mind that college wasn't for me. I wasn't sure that I could do it. I did not know about how I would pay for an education. Free Application for Federal Student Aid (FAFSA), federal loans, Pell grants, and other funding instruments were not talked about in my home. My mom was adamant about graduating high school, but she didn't push college. I didn't have the information enough to even dream.

My future husband had a great aunt named Evelyn. She was a great evangelist for higher education. She was a social worker with a Master's degree from Tennessee State University. While my boyfriend and I attended one of his family's weekly Sunday dinners, his great aunt invited us into an after-dinner conversation.

"We ought to get you back in school." I don't know what prompted the conversation, but she was unapologetic, straight forward, and confident. I was working at that time after graduating high school. I began with an explanation.

"Okay. I don't know. I'm working…"

"No. You can do it. They have programs for non-traditional students."

"I don't make a lot of money…" My fears sprang to the surface.

"No. You don't have to pay up front. You can get FAFSA and student loans."

"Won't that be debt?" At this point I was making excuses. I convinced myself that college was out of my reach for solid and defensible reasons.

"Everybody has student loans. It's okay. Some may even die with their loans, but an education is something they can't take away from you." She was like a salesperson or college recruiter. She would not take no for an answer. She was immune to my excuses.

"Okay. Get the application for me and I'll consider it." That was all she needed to hear.

The next Sunday, she couldn't wait to see me. She presented the application to me with a "thought I wouldn't" look on her face. I was hesitant.

"I don't know. The application is long, and I don't know about sitting in those 50-person classes."

"Okay. Maybe you can try Nashville State. The classes are smaller. It's a bit less expensive." She was undaunted and continue as if I had not provided a perfect roadblock. "What do you think you want to be?"

I couldn't answer right away still stunned that my roadblock had failed. She is a social worker. I remembered my mom talking to a social worker. I felt like I would like to help people. My mom and dad didn't marry until I was 9 years old. I remember when my name was changed. I remember my mother talking to a social worker for help with a few things related to the name change. "I don't know what I want to do exactly, but I think I want to be a social worker."

After that, it was a wrap. Before I knew what was happening, we had the application completed and I was in a line to meet with an advisor. That meeting seemed to confirm all my fears. I was slightly embarrassed, disappointed, and discouraged. The advisor informed me that I would have to take some classes that didn't matter toward the degree. The enrollment process included a test. The report came back with all the remediation that I needed. I was back in that space where I felt I was not smart enough. I remembered returning to my mom's house to pick up my daughter almost in tears, "I'm not smart enough."

I love my mother to this day for what she has consistently said to me throughout each of life's difficulties. Where she found the words, I don't know. How she knew they worked; I can't be sure. But every time she speaks life into me, I feel it like a defibrillator. "Go talk to them and see what you need to do. If you don't ask questions, you won't find out shit. I believe in you."

I went back to my husband's great aunt Evelyn and she was flippant, "Everybody has to take those classes. They may not tell you that they had to take them, but everyone has to take them." It took me back to what my mother said. *No questions, you won't find out.* I immediately felt like I was not alone. I felt inspired. I felt relief. I was excited, nervous, and anxious. I need to hear that because I was back in that place. Her words combined with my mother's encouragement lifted a weight off me.

The highlights on the sheet were discouraging. I couldn't see how I was going to take the remediation and take all the other classes I needed to take for my major. It was a learning curve for me. I had not been in this environment before. But I had a supportive circle that I had demonstrated their worth. I knew I could count on them to help me complete this journey.

Legacy

It was a huge deal to go to Nashville State Community College, graduate, and apply to Tennessee State University (TSU). I went on to complete TSU as well. As I sit to write this book, I am the only one in my family who has a bachelor's degree. I graduated in 2017 and advanced in my career. My hope is to inspire any woman or man that has a background like mine to find the courage to believe in yourself. I hope to provide in these words the same encouragement that my husband's great aunt empowered me with. "You can do this. College is for you. You can start and you can complete."

My daughter started Nashville State Community College right after high school. I was happy to tell her everything about the experience. I felt a great sense of pride being able to share the experience with her as she walked in the same halls that I walked. I got to share in the same feelings she felt as a new student; uncertain, unsettled, yet curious and hopeful.

In her senior year, we discussed college. She went through a period of crying and upset because she didn't know what she wanted to do with her life.

"I don't know what I want to do. I just know that I want to deal with the mind." I remembered telling Terence's great aunt the same thing. Her advice to me was, "Start. You will figure it out." That's the same advice that I gave my daughter. I encouraged her that she could do whatever she wanted.

"Take your time. Start. Take the classes that you feel comfortable with." She was concerned about falling behind her friends who were taking 5 classes on a full-ride scholarship.

"I don't know if I can do that." We sat down with the course plan and orchestrated our own plan that she felt comfortable with. Her anxiety reduced tremendously.

I accept the role Terence's great aunt was for me. I am a cheerleader and a translator. When she has an assignment that she dreads, I encourage and communicate the requirements in a simpler form.

"Just do it! They're asking you what you got out of it. Remember, you want to *deal with the mind*!" I repeat in a mimicking way because she said she enjoys her Psychology class. I enjoy being able to communicate with her from a position of knowing. I often communicate the importance of just completing your assignments and the why. The reasons for the assignment and how they relate to the learning are the most critical to motivation. I also find that joking about it works as well. It seems to take the stress away. One minute she is stressing. The next she can laugh. That's my advice to anyone who is dreading the start or wondering about the why of continuing. Just do it. Completing is a reward you can't fully appreciate until you cross the finish line.

Wanting a Legacy for You

If you want to create a legacy that honors your parents and caregivers and provides a foundation for those who come after you, I say go for it. Don't allow fear, lack of knowledge, or other obstacles to keep you from it. It is not easy. It will not always look pretty. In fact, it will look ugly at times. But the reward is better than you dream. You only remember the pain as it helps you to empathize and help those that come after you. You will be able to share in their journey and be a reason they persevere.

Chapter 2: Housing Projects & Stigma

Maybe eighth grade, I saw the importance of my family unit. I could see why my parents didn't want us in certain places or out after certain times. We heard about the occurrences in the neighborhood where we lived. With more frequency that was comfortable, someone in the neighborhood would be shot or land in trouble with the legal system. Despite the dangers I understood, I wanted more freedom or at least a loosening of the reins.

Stigma

People looked down on us because of where we lived. We were not expected to achieve much. We lived in the projects, subsidized housing. Even after we moved into home away from the housing development, people judged us by where we came from.

It didn't occur to me as a problem to be solved. We lived where we lived. A two-bedroom apartment was made to be home. People may have had their preconceptions about the environment. But it was home. You may have people living next to you who weren't as clean as you were. But my parents were clean. My father was clean to a fault. We could not eat in our rooms. Any critters that would wander into our apartment would not find anything to eat.

We had a good time in the homes. We could go out and play with our friends. We ate as a family every night. People looked out for each other generally. There was a rough end of the housing development over where the three bedrooms were, but my parents made the best of the living conditions. I felt safe. Shooting was normal in the vicinity, but I did not feel unsafe. I remember being annoyed that my parents had us come in when there were shots fired. I never felt scared.

We had a field nearby. We just called it *the field*. I don't know what was going on up there, but that's where the killing happened. Fights were common, but people were able to let it go and move on. Retaliation was low. People would do anything for a high or an escape even if it was temporary.

As a pre-teen, I had the distinct feeling that I was looked down upon by people who didn't live in the projects. I had a couple of friends who didn't live in the projects that couldn't stay the night at my house. I was not invited to stay over their houses either.

My peers judged themselves to be less than because of where they came from as well. They often did not think they could be college educated. It wasn't talked about. The goal was to get a good job and make some money. The conversation was not about higher education. It was almost like someone was waiting on the next person to bring up the future and opportunities.

We had a normal routine. We would go to school. Come home, complete homework, and go back outside. The experience my parents provided was structured and loving. They always instilled that they wanted better for us. They were showing us by example as well. They emphasized that we did not have to be a product of our environment. Our futures were not determined by where we lived.

I feel like I can deal with everything based on the experience growing up. Even shooting doesn't bother me. An incident would have to be in proximity. I would have to see the gun to be bothered. I still visit there from time to time. I know what I can and can't do, where I can and cannot go. I know what times are witching and which are not. A different generation of residents exists today. A different group of people with a seemingly different value base are present now. The support system may not have been as stable for this generation as I experienced. Yet I don't judge. I just recognize that it is different. My mom and dad made the difference. I didn't know I was poor. I always had food, a listening ear, and the expectation that I could be better.

Moving on Up

I was in the 8th grade when my parents moved out of the housing projects and bought a house. Middle School at that time was only 7th & 8th grade. I remember my mom and dad's conversation about the impending rent increase. The annual income and asset review meant a tremendous increase in rent. They knew they had to do something else. The perception is that people in the projects don't work. But if they work and do well, they run the risk of being priced out of the housing. That's what happened to my parents. My father worked for a man who purchased a home and allowed my parents to rent to own. The man knew my father's situation and his work ethic.

The place was filthy when we first viewed the property. It was a foreclosure. The home needed a lot of work. The family that lived there before allowed the place to deteriorate. We set a few pest-control bombs. It didn't have central air and heating. My father picked up a second job at Red Lobster to afford ceiling fans for the rooms in the Summer. We used kerosene heaters in the Winter. The hardest part was Summers spent washing walls and ceiling fans because of the kerosene heaters. Yet it was a bonding experience for the whole family. I always think about that experience and feel gratitude when I think about the comforts I enjoy now like central air, a dishwasher, and ceiling fans. I still have the habit of washing dishes in the sink rather than using the dishwasher.

My sisters and I were saddened because we were leaving our friends. We eventually learned to enjoy the experience. We upgraded to larger bikes and stored them in our new backyard. We had a sidewalk to ride on as opposed to a parking lot. My parents made it comfortable by keeping us in the same schools. We were able to keep our interactions with our friends.

The neighborhood wasn't much better than the one we moved from. Our bikes were stolen from the backyard. But it was a house that we could call our own. No neighbors with their pest control issues to contend with. We came home after that and a fence was fortified with chains. The windows were completed with burglar bars.

The house had three bedrooms. My older sisters shared a room because they were closer in age. I had my own room until my sister got pregnant. My middle sister was pregnant at 16. She was looked down upon. My parents were upset at first, but they quickly reset to ensure that she could complete school.

She was an inspiration to me. She was determined that she was not going to be what the outsiders said she would be. She wasn't going to be a high school dropout. My parents took up another night office building cleaning job to help pay for day care. I remember my sister and my mother crying about people who turned away, shamed my sister, and talked about my mother because of the pregnancy. It hurt because it came from people we knew. She proved them all wrong by working hard and completing her high school diploma on time.

The University

Tennessee State University (TSU) was close to where we lived. TSU was a "Black school," a historically black college or university (HBCU) to be exact. People I knew were interested in the institution because of that connection. We would travel down Murfreesboro Pike to Rosa Parks Blvd and the Farmer's Market. I would see the TSU downtown campus. We had friends who lived nearer the main campus. We would pass it and I would be intimidated. I never thought I was smart enough to go to TSU. So many cars in the parking lot, such long lines, so much happening. I knew it was a university. That meant a sea of people. We were brought up to graduate high school and get a good job. In my mind, I was focused on the job search after graduation.

The newspaper was the way to find work. When my first sister graduated, she told me that she would look in the paper and search under "General." Maybe it was because she didn't have work experience. Maybe it was because she needed work experience. That's what I thought I would do. It took me a while to figure out another way. I am not sure who told me, but someone suggested that I look in other areas. I looked through call centers advertisements and customer service position announcements. I knew I wanted to do something in office work, but beyond that I was unsure.

When I was thinking about a job only, I had a whisper of a feeling that I needed something more under my belt than a high school diploma. I understood that I could ask questions. My mother always repeated, *If you don't ask questions, you don't get answers*. I was still hesitant because I didn't want to come across as the dumb girl from the projects.

As I matured, I realized that people only know what you tell them. I wish I had come to that realization sooner. College was a leap of faith. I had a lot of anxiety by the time I got to TSU. There were younger people and I didn't know what to expect. If I saw someone closer to my age, I felt a bit more comfortable. I would enter classes and quietly take my seat. The syllabus was intimidating. I would ask my questions after class not wanting to ask aloud in front of the class. I felt like every class was different and required different skills of me. That persisted until I got into classes related to my major. Math classes were horrible because I remembered my anxiety and frustrations with Algebra from high school. I could feel like I knew the material I studied, but the anxiety left me blank.

In the process, I learned that I can complete what I start. I must calm down and take care of myself. My greatest challenge to overcome was overthinking. Each semester, I would hype myself up with uncertainty about the teachers, the assignments, and any other differences. I didn't want to be the person raising her hand met with, "Oh, her again." I was sure that they would not babysit or hand hold me, but I wished they would be more intentional about inviting questions and engaging the comfortability of the students. I adopted a pattern of self-calming that built as I was successful. I told myself that I could do it because I did it the previous semester.

Wanting More than Stigma for You

Living in the projects was not source of concern for me. I was more concerned about our family and our interactions. I learned a deep desire to nurture family with passion, showing up, and understanding. I hold those values to this day. Where you come from is neither hindrance nor excuse. You bring your destiny to pass by your decisions. Always guard your choice.

My sister's experience taught me about working for what you wanted to achieve. I would wake up in the night to get water and pass my sister's room. I saw her up late working on assignments she needed to complete. You can achieve anything you are willing to put the work into. Learn how, connect to get access, and work. You will get there.

My sister's pregnancy also taught me never to judge anyone. I refuse to look down on someone. I don't know their situation. I don't know their story. Both experiences remind me to humble myself. When I find myself judging even for a second, I quickly reset and re-member two things. First, it is rough out here for everyone. People are left in situations that are out of their control. Second, many if given the chance to do it over would make different choices. We have all made choices that we wish we could take back. Don't let that hold you back. Don't bow to stigma. Allow the experience to remind you to support others toward second chances.

Chapter 3: The Start

Movies and television shows can suggest that you can be better but doing better is a personal responsibility. Leaving the nest is already fearful, but not having the means can be a source of worry for a person. You know enough to know that so much exists that you don't know. This is where you need the internal push to ask questions and seek help. This book is an example. I have wanted to write a book for a long time. I didn't know anything about the process. I didn't know what I would write, what I would say. I hesitated because of this. My experience was limited. Yet I decided that it was something I would do. I made a clear pronouncement that I wanted to achieve this goal. I reached out to someone who could help me order my thoughts. I connected with the help I needed to get it done.

Is it Fear?

The perception is that people in the projects don't work. In the projects, you don't have a light bill. You don't have to take care of a water bill, landscaping, or repairs. You also have low rent if any rent. That stereotype about work breeds low expectations and limits your dreams. Add to that the fact that adulthood brings with it a ton of responsibilities outside of the housing projects or whatever is your comfort zone. The basic fear everyone has is of being independent, left to answer for yourself and your choices without mom and dad to back you up.

I remember one friend of mine. Her mom was addicted to drugs at a time when little help was available in the community. She had to grow up quickly and care for siblings and herself. She didn't have the push of someone in the home. She could have easily made poor choices and blamed her situation as the cause. But she didn't. Despite the perception others placed upon her and the circumstances she had to endure, she persevered. The fear she held had to give way to her desire for more. She had no other option, in her mind, but to make it work.

I had two parents in my home. My parents had two incomes. We faced other pressures, but our home was stable. I was a dreamer with the luxury of fear. Whereas my friend had nothing to lose, I saw that I had something of value in my family.

I kept a diary as a younger girl. I wrote about what I would see in my experiences during middle school. I wrote what I wanted my life to look like as an adult. It was scary because the future held a great amount of uncertainty. I was just a young girl. Was I worthy of the dreams I had? I was also fearful of failure. I would think that I was not able to do it. I was worried about people talking and embarrassing me about my failures. I always wanted a husband, a house, and two children. I saw positive shows on television that allowed me to dream those dreams. I am thankful that I have achieved much of what I dreamed about. There were times when I didn't think it was going to happen, but I kept moving.

Encouragement can be a whisper every day that reminds you that everything will work out. For me, I trained my mind over time by encouraging myself. Each day, I told myself, *It is okay if it doesn't work out.* I developed a dialogue within myself that was a discussion about what I wanted. If I wanted it, I had to realize that I must go after it. Whether two parents, one, or none the reality doesn't change unless I put in the work. Whether fearful or not, I too had no other option but to make it work.

I had to return to my faith. This included going back to the Bible. Interesting fun fact: my grandmother and I were baptized at the same time. I gained a view and practice of spirituality from church attendance and communications with my grandmother. I learned to have the faith of a mustard seed. My father held that loyalty was paramount. Your word should be your bond. Gain the things that people can't take away from you. Your determination is what propels you to your goals. If you are going to get it, you must really want it. If it doesn't work out, there is a bigger plan. God has a plan that is working for me.

Generational Curses

Yet, I'm not perfect. I think my husband and I had a curse to break for our lives. Both our parents gave birth to us at a young age. We were able to wait until age 21 for our first child. I was able to graduate from a community college and a university without an example in my family. I could look to my husband's family, but not my own.

I am looked at as the strong sister and daughter. I could not fail in the eyes of my family because they need my strength. That is how I thought. I realize that I was the "Yes-Girl." I did a lot of things I didn't want to do because I wanted people to like me. I'm reminded of an adage that says, "If you say no or go broke, you will see who genuinely accepts you." I found that I received less initially when I dropped the ball as the Yes-Girl. But that initial loss allowed others to pick up more of the burden.

In my maturity, I have come to the place where I am more comfortable saying no, limiting my exposure, and scheduling according to my needs. I have learned to focus on self-care. I had to realize that I was most important. I had to realize that I was first. My peace of mind, my health is first. I now understand that you are liked more when you put yourself first and set boundaries that work for you. When people stop wholly depending on you, it's a relief. People really can do things without you when you let them.

I am still that stereotypical strong Black woman in many ways. But I also have the most supportive family and husband anyone could ask for. I don't ordinarily share when I am down or depressed. The only person who knows those struggles is my husband, Terence. He knew from the beginning that I was nervous and a worrier. He knew that I would have to go to the bathroom when I was nervous. Early on in our relationship, he learned to encourage me. His encouragement rubbed off on me, and I remembered to encourage myself. I have learned to focus on the development, both individual and collective. I have settled into a pattern of self-encouragement. I had decided to leave their thoughts (even supportive people) out of my equation. In this way, I resist any anxiety that can come from the outside.

I am sure that we have addressed some generational curses in our own lives. But our greatest evidence is our daughters. For me, my role is to educate my daughters sooner rather than later. I received information later in life and through trial and error. I am educating them on finances, home buying, and college education. There is more out there. You don't have to be afraid of the unknown. Travel is one example. I took them to Disney World. It was the first time I had ever been. I want them to see more of the world than I saw growing up. I want the world to seem smaller in their eyes than I saw it when I was a child. I went to an majority Black school growing up. My daughter's school and our neighborhood are more diverse. You learn from different cultures and experiences with other backgrounds. My husband is big on taking our daughters out to dine in restaurants with white tablecloths. He often seriously jokes that he doesn't want any guys thinking that they are doing them any favors. They can't do anything for them that they have not been exposed to. That exposure is important.

Reliance versus Resilience

Of course, we all need income. You may love or like that job, but that is not the only job. I would talk about my struggles in the housing project. My husband never lived in that environment, but he said, "I understand struggle. I know what that's like. I have to be a man and go out here and get it for my family." If one job is lost, you need to go and get another one. By the same token, you must see work as work toward a paycheck.

The tension is reliance versus resilience. Reliance is trust in someone or something. You feel this when you have a foundation to work from, people to lean on, and a pattern to follow. I felt this sense of reliance as I watched my parents work and listened to their guidance. Yet each of us must grow up and stand on our own two feet. My husband was not going to take away my responsibility for myself and my growth and my maturity. I can trust him, not become codependent.

Resilience is the ability to overcome setbacks and deficits resulting from several factors. You express resilience when you, like my friend, can still achieve even with a mother who is hooked on drugs. I felt this having come from the projects. Rather than accepting what others thought and projected, I dreamed a dream for myself. The danger is to forget the work involved and seek the appearance rather than the protective factors. Don't allow doing better to write checks that you can't cash.

My husband taught this to me when we were looking to purchase our first home. He kept that balance of reliance and resilience in front of me. This new chapter was not about getting the best and the most expensive. It is not about maxing our budget and biting off more than we could chew. It was about being able to take care of what we purchased.

My husband and I balance each other. He's the numbers person. He is better with money. He negotiated the purchase price for our house. He is my encourager. He has always told me that I could do it whatever it is. When I talked about going to school, he was matter of fact.

"Babe, I don't know if I can do it. I know you are used to having me do certain things around the house and taking care of..."

"Baby, we'll figure it out." He is just a positive person. His encouragement came from his great grandmother. His grandmother raised him. He is gifted with elder wisdom gained from her. I often tell him that he was raised as an old man.

We started from different places, but both were challenging. We trusted each other. We grew together. We share the lessons and the fruits of that growth with our daughters. We often go back to the compromising skill that we learned in marriage counseling. We respect each other in communication, time, and schedule. This is what makes it work.

Wanting to Start for You

Just because you start in a place doesn't mean that you end there. You don't have to be a product of your environment. Growing up in the projects, in the household of my parents, made me the person that I am. But I also had a part to play. I had to decide that I was going to do what it took to succeed. I had to push past the fear and decide that success was my only option. Along the way, I accepted that things may not always work out. I learned to encourage myself. These are lessons for you as well.

Whoever you are or decide to be, know that you can survive. You know the survival and the tools that you need. You will be able to make it in any situation. You can also thrive when you dream beyond your circumstance and put in the work. And never forget that your worst day is only one day in many more to come. My husband once said to me, "Some people really lose it if they lose something. You just learn how to make it when you grew up like us." Take it from me, don't lose it! If you choose to step out here simply because you want better, you will make it. You will find the tools and the opportunities that are needed as you go. You may not have it all before you start. Just start.

Section II: A Rose from Concrete

Chapter 4: High School Psalm

My Experience

Moving into high school was exciting for me. My sisters told grand stories about their experiences. I was a bit fearful about the transition, but I had them for support. It would be the first time since elementary school that I would attend with both my sisters. They prepared me for the experience throughout the Summer leading up to my first day. What to wear and what not to wear. Who to stay away from and who was interesting. What classes to take and which to steer clear of. Protecting myself was important.

My parents liked that we were riding the same bus. Their advice was to be myself and not get caught up into trouble and delinquency. I remember my first day. The school was so big. Many students would skip class. We participated in the activity as well. I remember we skipped class once and visited another high school. That was the nature of high school in those days. Autonomy was the norm.

I was a bad ass. I must admit. I knew I had to protect me. I didn't bother anyone, but I would not take anything either. My sisters were the same way. Mom gave us specific instructions. "If one fights, you all fight. Don't let anyone walk over you. Say what's on your mind." It wasn't because of her advice, but we got into 3 fights that established our reputation as a family that should not be taken lightly. We were known as the Archibald girls. They knew we wouldn't take anything from anyone. They knew that if they said something smart, they would have to answer for it. If they decided to take a swing, all 3 girls would be involved in the scuffle.

I got into a lot of fights because I didn't take anything from anyone. That's the environment I came from. I was nothing to play with. I was set on survival. I would take things personal. I remember one incident. Some girl was talking crazy on the bus. "Who you talking to?" My sister wasn't there. A girl was talking crazy.

"All of ya'll!" I was always taught to respect myself and cause people to respect me.

"Who are you talking to?" I was not going to allow someone to punk me. I didn't want them to think they could talk and think that I wasn't going to do anything. You had to take up for yourself. If you stood up to the worst one in the group, the others would back down and you would earn respect. That's just how it was.

Defending my honor was one memory. The extracurricular activities were another. The pep rallies were grand. The basketball games were fun when we could go. I remember the homecoming games most. Everyone talked about it the whole day daydreaming aloud about what they were going to wear. My sisters competed for the mirror trying on different outfits. My mom dropped us off at the game. We sat at the top of the bleachers. We had the one friend who brought makeup so that we could get more made up.

Krystal's hamburger was the spot to go after the game. We called my mom to let her know what we were doing afterward. She wasn't comfortable because it was her job to go and tell my dad. We didn't have the same concerns then that we have now. No seatbelts. We just piled about 6 or 7 deep in a 5 seater car. After Krystal's it was off to make curfew.

Senior Year

My sisters graduated in order before me. We graduated 1993, 1994, and 1995. I didn't have my sister's senior year. And I needed them. It was rough. In my senior Year of High School, my parents divorced.

We could pick electives. I worked toward cosmetology for the first 3 years of high school. It was a stress-reliever for me. I loved making people feel pretty. When you look good, you feel good. I must have been good at it. People would request me for services. The course allowed me to cover two course periods. As a senior, it was 3 periods. I accumulated credits throughout the year. The credits from high school would roll over into a cosmetology school if I wished even if I did not finish in high school. All that would be left is to complete a board examination and I could be licensed. I was fortunate because all schools did not have the elective.

My cosmetology teacher would put up flyers everywhere. People would come in one way and leave better than they imagined. We were a full-service salon. Hair, makeup, pedicures, and manicures. I drew a line in the sand when it came touching people's feet. I didn't want to perform pedicures until my teacher put it in a different perspective. She told me that the feet are cleaner than the hands. It made sense to me and the hesitation was overcome.

Even with all that accomplished and the reputation I gained; I gave it up in my senior year. I reached a point where I didn't want to do it anymore. I lost my patience for listening to the indecisiveness of clients. I knew that patience was a requirement. If a client did not like their style, I would have to make it right. I just didn't want to go through it anymore.

I stopped, but my cousin Shawnta says she took up cosmetology because of my example. She is now a successful hair salon owner. I could not be prouder.

I lost interest in a lot of things during that year. Reading was a passion of mine up until that time. I would read thrillers and love stories mostly. Even that fell victim to my home situation.

I had exams to go through. I didn't want my situation to affect my prospects for graduation. I knew about my parents and the hard time they were having. I was the go-between. I told him things that she wanted him to know. I told her things that he wanted her to know. I felt like it was better in the projects. We ate together. It was more of a family time. We communicated more. I don't know if it was moving to a house or us getting older, but there was a difference. Being the youngest, a lot was hidden from me. But, when my sisters moved out, I began to see the change in my parent's relationship. There was a vibe in the house that was different. My mom was always the supportive mom, but I knew something was changing. Senior year is when the communication through me created. "Ask your dad about that." "Go take that up with your momma." I remember talking to my sisters and wondering if they were going to make it. I did not know it at the time, but my mother had already made her decision. She was waiting for me to graduate. Her promise to me was the only thing keeping her from moving.

Meanwhile, I had to humble myself. I had a class that was becoming a problem and a potential barrier to my graduation. I wanted to pass the class above all. I had to consider the good along with the bad. I had to consider that there was more good than bad. Overwhelmed, I went to my grandmother for guidance. My grandmother spent some time and talked with me. She always made sense, but I needed this moment more than any other. She told me, "Read the

23 Psalm." I felt a relief after I talked to her. She always gave a lot of wisdom. I read and memorized the 23 Psalm. I recited it all the way to my exams and passed.

My mother moved out of our home and into a 2-bedroom apartment. She told me right after the Christmas break. My dad went to work one day, and my uncles arrived and began to pack. My two older sisters had already left. I knew my mom was happy about her choice to divorce. My sisters and I felt that it was the best thing. While they lived together, neither of them was happy. Moving out was a happiness to both. To make ends meet in this new living situation, my mom picked up extra hours at a 24-hour facility for the developmentally deficient.

Relationships

I wanted to be with my friends. I met my boyfriend at the time. His name was Terence. I met him over the Summer. We both had a knack for socializing with other people. The games were the talk of the school. Whose dating who and all the gossip was important to the high school experience. I would get to spend time with him at the games. I knew he would come to the games. I was focused on getting to know him.

My mom was the talkative parent when it came to the topic of boys. She was a straight shooter. She didn't sugar coat. My older sisters had boyfriends. They would offer their advice as well about guys and dating. I was the teenager who wanted to experience the teenage life. Socializing was life.

Most of my friends had boyfriends, so I wanted that friend that is also a boy that I could connect with. I had friends who were in different stages of relationships. I wasn't ready for more than just kissing. I was interested in Prom. I looked forward to it. We attended junior and senior year.

I felt like I was grown. I was 18 and I graduated. I had a boy-friend who seemed to be a keeper. I started at a Dry-Cleaning outfit right after high school as a cashier. Things were going well.

Terence didn't see a problem or say anything, but I felt like I wasn't spending enough time with him. I felt like I needed to spend more time with my mother. I didn't want her to be alone. She is a strong woman who doesn't say much. You must pull it out of her if you need to know. My nephew lived with us part-time. He would hang with his mother periodically, but he was so used to my mother that he stayed with her often. Along with feeling grown, I was begin-ning to feel ready for my next level up.

Wanting a Psalm for You

High school was tough for me. My parents divorce was form-ative in my development, but I will always be grateful for how my parents handled it. They never broke their promise to get my sisters and I through high school. To that point, life was about finishing high school and respecting myself, which also included requiring others to do the same. As I focused on the task at hand, I learned the power of faith and gained a verse to own throughout my challenges. I chal-lenge you to read the 23rd Psalm and make the connections, feel the encouragement, and live the promises. With multiple requirements on your time and person, with life always poised to throw you an-other curve ball, you must be certain that it will always work out. Though you walk even through the valley of the shadow of death, don't fear evil. Your table is prepared, and your enemies can't stop you from receiving the blessing that is promised to you.

Chapter 5: Defining More

My first job was as a cashier at a dry cleaner. My dad was still around. I would call him for money, but I needed my own money. I wanted to buy my own clothes and shoes. I was into fashion. I wanted to get my hair done at the beauty parlor. I also wanted to help my mother. I wanted her to be able to go out to eat occasionally. That was partly for me as well. I wanted something different than what was cooked.

My Independence

I feel like I had to grow up fast. After my sister gave birth at 16, the baby was everyone's baby. I had to become a parent as well. I wanted independence. I heard my parent's voice in my ear. I knew that there were certain things I would need if I would have what I wanted. Chief among these needs was a job and a car.

I had a strong relationship with Terence's grandmother. His family accepted me with open arms. Terence's grandmother co-signed for me to buy a 1992 Honda Civic. She saw something in me. Maybe she saw something that I didn't see at that time. I think she saw a person who wanted something better for herself. We would sit on her wrap-around porch and talk. She was a talker. We would discuss the future, my determination, my desire to make it. I will never forget where I came from, but I knew that I didn't want to go backward. My family strength gave me a sense of my ability to figure it out and survive no matter what. It may have been that the examples and a specific hand up came from Terence's family.

Now, I had a car note and insurance payment. I felt pressure due to having a co-signer. Over time, I wanted more. I would look periodically for a new job. The cashier position was fine for the moment, but it was not what I wanted to do. I thought I couldn't get to where I wanted to go unless I did something else. Every time I found a job that looked interesting, they wanted a bachelor's degree. I didn't even have a resume.

I continued to look until I found an ad for a file clerk at an insurance company. I dressed the best I could. I didn't have a lot of professional clothes. I didn't know what to expect from an office job. I was intimidated by that. I felt like it was a more serious job. I interviewed and had the job the first day. They had not had a file clerk for a while. I had a job to do, but it was something I was ready for.

After 6 months, my probation period was over. I made friends with a co-worker who was in the customer service area of the business. It was a small call-center style set up. The job was answering phones and placing some outgoing calls. An opening was advertised for a position in her shop.

"You should apply," she suggested.

"What do you have to have? I don't have any experience and just my high school diploma." I was hesitant, but knew it was an increase in pay. The phones were intimidating to me because I was not familiar with that.

"You don't need anything. They will train you. I'm going to put in a good word for you." Even though I was intimidated, afraid, and unsure, I still had to go for it. It was a leap of faith. *You have to ask.*

They can say Yea or Nay. I could almost hear my mother's words. I took a chance because all they could do is tell me no. I almost counted myself out, but I'm glad I didn't. I applied. I interviewed. I got the job. I was in disbelief. I moved seamlessly into the position in customer service at the company. It was the office job that I had always wanted. I had a little space where I could put the picture of my family up. I was more excited to come to work. I was around people, totally different from the file room.

My mother was extremely proud when I told her. "What? You have a desk job!" It was as if a goal had come to fruition for us both.

From there, my work history was a series of advancements and increases in pay. I learned much during this time about the realities of work and the value of a health and progressive work environment. It was 1997 when I started at the Insurance Company. By 2002, I worked with a lot of social workers at Family and Children's Services. I enjoyed seeing people come in and watching as their lives were changed. This was about the time I had a spark toward wanting to do something else.

Courage & Encouragement

I started at Nashville State Community College in 2010. I started school just before I was laid off from Family and Children's Services. School reimbursement was available up to a limit of $500. You had to write an essay and show your transcript. Once approved, you received a check for $500. Some classes made me want to quit. But I leaned on my determination. I knew this was what I had to do to get further in life and the work world.

Some people can't see anything more than what they have in front of them. I don't know where strength gets worn down. But it seems that relationships make a difference. I had one girl say something about mating and husband requirements. Her requirement included that her husband could not be a tradesman or work in anything other than a job where he wore a suit and tie. I never had that requirement, nor do I believe in such foolishness.

My father would always talk about "working hands. That's what you want to see on a man." What he meant was that a man ought to work. You see the evidence of his work when you look at his hands. What it means for me is that marriage is about work between two committed people. When you want to know whether they are progressing together, look at them together. Ask them about their happiness and their joy in life. When it comes to men, ask whether they are supportive first, responsive second, and consistent always.

I remind my daughter of the example that her father is. He did not pursue education. He pursued what he enjoyed. My husband worked as a custodian for years. That income afforded us a nice lifestyle. I have never been ashamed of our progress or our work ethic. I don't even worry with those things. He enjoys the work he does. He makes choices based on his enjoyment and sense of progress for the family rather than what others may think. Terence always like to clean.

When the job at the car lot was not making our ends meet, he worked to get something that fit. When it came to my desire for education, he was all in. When I wanted to quit, he encouraged me to stick with it. When I hesitated, he was a rock of consistency and support.

My daughter had a boyfriend once. I noticed that her first boyfriend was attempting to isolate her. He was controlling and going through her phone. I encourage her toward healthy relationships like that her dad demonstrates to her daily. I tell her to know her worth. I tell her to know that she is worthy of her dreams and refuse any man who will attempt to convince her otherwise.

Being Optimistic

I went to a healing retreat and was asked about the core values that make life worthwhile. I thought about it in the context of my desire throughout my life to advance, gain, and achieve more. I asked my self where the motivation came from. I wondered how to put into words the values that were instilled within me as a child growing up where I grew up.

Will. My first value is will. My parents used the resources that they knew. They used our situations growing up as steppingstones. Whether it was living in the projects, working multiple jobs, or enduring the challenges of high school, the will must be present to be clear that the current position is not the final position. This is not where I want to stay. I want more and I can have more.

Resources. The second value I would list is resources. Maybe people think they don't have the means, or they don't recognize how to navigate the systems. Maybe they don't have anybody they can count on for an example or a hand up. I encourage you to change your perspective if this is you. Rather than thinking about the resources you don't have, start with what you do have. Even if all you have is the desire to do better, that is enough to get you to the next task. Look for people who can give you information. Ask questions. Refuse embarrassment and the fear of looking out of place. You can do everything you have the audacity to dream. I don't know if people hear that enough.

Learning. Ask what you need to achieve the goals. Then, commit yourself to finding them and learning about them. Even if you don't have $1 million dollars, you can learn about financial literacy and wealth creation. Public libraries are still free to browse. Read the books available. Ask for suggestions from the librarian. Use the computers and the Internet. You can get the information you need even if you aren't enrolled in a school.

Happiness. Your happiness is the chief matter in life. Learn all that you can learn. Self-respect is important. Meaningful work is critical. My husband has exemplified what it means to be a committed husband and a great father. He has also demonstrated happiness by example. Do what you love, and you may work. But the life you create is full of joy.

Community. Community is a large part of my story and a value that I hold to this day. I am who I am because of where I came from. From my home, to my neighborhood, to my in-laws, to school-teachers, co-workers, and friends I am filled with gratitude. I have been shaped by all of them. And, I'm not done.

Be Your Best. Value your best. Keep going. Sum it up with not giving up. Reflecting on the number of times I wanted to give up reminds that I am human. Reflecting on the support and encouragement that saw me through increases my confidence. I share with my daughters the foundation they have in their father and me. I will tell anyone who will listen that making it is up to you. Be your best even before you commit to doing your best. The reward comes from consistently being. See it to the end. Everything works out in the end. If it hasn't worked out, it isn't the end.

Defining More for You

I am not interested in telling you who to marry or what person is good for you, but I will impress upon you the value of relationships when you consider how you will progress in life. Your success begins with a definition of More for you. Listen to the positive advice and encouragement that you receive from others including those outside your family. Look at the positive examples you have around you even outside of your immediate family. Resist the negative, naysayers, no-goers, and never-wents in your world. They have standards that are about appearances and pretense rather than substance and truth. Know that your most important resources are the people that you invite and allow into your life. When you choose solid people, they are a foundation that you can build additional dreams upon.

Chapter 6: Growing Up

Terence and I talked about having a family and having our own place early on. We were young, so those conversations seemed more like dreams than plans. We knew that we would be together forever. We were grown. We were a team, but I was afraid of marriage. I saw it as a huge responsibility. Of course, a baby is a responsibility as well, but marriage was different somehow. We both agreed that we didn't want to get married right away. No one in my family was married before kids. It wasn't stressed to us. Having kids at an early age was discussed often. The message was Don't. But marriage wasn't talked about. We were both from families that birthed children early. My mother was always a proponent of birth control. She knew my sister took me to Planned Parenthood.

"Let's have a baby!" We both agreed. We didn't have a good job, but it was a logical move that we planned. We didn't get pregnant right away. We tried for some time. And, it happened!

I missed my cycle and we made a doctor's appointment for testing. The clinic gave us papers with information and a proposed due date. Terence came home with me and delivered the papers to my mother. She took the news as I expected. I was out of high school. Terence was my high school sweetheart. This was a logical step in maturation.

My mother sat me down after Terence went home. She asked me what I wanted. She has always been emotionally intelligent. She wanted to make sure that I had a voice and the freedom to make my own decisions. I told her of our plans. The discussion seemed to satisfy her questions.

Meanwhile, I was fearful. I worried about whether I would be a good mother. I was concerned that we were not financially stable. I questions how we would afford to give her the things I wanted to give her. At the age of 21, I was pregnant with my first daughter. I was living with my mother. Her father was living with his grandmother.

My daughter was born, and we continued to cycle between both living spaces. We had more space in Terence's room. My mom had a boyfriend at the time that she eventually married. He and my mom were great. I had some issues after the pregnancy that necessitated my mother stepping in. I am forever grateful.

A Decision to Grow Up

As my daughter grew, we were recognizing a need for more space. We decided that we needed our own space. Terence, at the time, was cleaning cars on the car lot. I was working in a dry cleaner. We needed better jobs. That was a fear of trying to establish credit and get our own place. We talked to Terence's grandmother. She co-signed for the townhouse. We rented a two-bedroom townhouse for $525. We moved in together, and though we had been together for a while, living together was different.

We were young. Our relationship wasn't perfect. We were both on board with what we wanted. We just lived a lifestyle that was "grown" but not "grown up." We went out with friends. Terence with his boys and me with my girls. My husband had a few friends who were victims of homicide. Life was happening around us. We were forced to contemplate life. We had to do the right thing for our child. It wasn't just about us anymore. We sat down and decided that we had to act like parents. We had to admit that we were acting like teenagers. It wasn't just the going out. It was the sense of separateness.

As I look back, I recognize the difference between marriage and single. The connection you have with your husband is different than that you have with the best of boyfriends. The sense of building, working together, considering one another is different. It holds more weight and simultaneously release some weights. I can admit to some jealousy when Terence would go out. He was popular out in the streets! I had some feelings about his comings and goings. But we both had a moment where we connected with clarity and decided to grow up. It was a challenge to let go of our youthful selves. We had to do better.

The Proposal

It was 2004. It was my birthday. I was turning 27. Terence took me to Kobe Steakhouse under the guise of a birthday dinner. We walked out of the steakhouse and a limousine was waiting for us.

"What is this?" I looked at Terence.

"This is our ride." We stepped into the limousine while I was still perplexed. He grabbed my hand while sitting on the seat. "I just want to wish you a happy birthday. I love you. We have a beautiful daughter together. I want to spend the rest of my life with you." He got on one knee while in the limousine and proposed. "Will you marry me?" I said Yes through my tears of joy and surprise.

My great aunt, Martha, really loved Terence. We called her Pee Wee. She was the fancy aunt. She smoked long cigarettes. Pee Wee always said that Terence and I would be married. She passed away about a month prior to her pronouncement coming true. I thought about her immediately after I said Yes. My tears of joy were mingled with the thought of my great aunt. I was marrying my high school sweetheart!

Terence had told me that he was taking my graduation gift rings to get them cleaned. It was a two-ring set. He got the two rings soldered together to create our proposal ring.

I can't say that it started with that decision, but the decision to grow up was an important moment for us. From there, my perspective was opened to the possibilities. I wanted more. The space for my daughter to play. Her own room. I wanted to be married. She deserved more. I deserved more. My mother had me at 18. She had other children at 15 and 16. Her mother was the same. They had not completed high school. They pushed me to desire more for myself.

We married and almost immediately talked about having another baby. It didn't take long for us to get pregnant with a second child. It turned out to be a less than ideal time. My father was in the hospital for a major surgery. I was splitting time between visits to the hospital, work, and taking care of home. We found out on one visit that he was bleeding in intensive care. It was a lot of stress. While this was being revealed, Terence hurt himself. He had a schedule hernia surgery two days after my father's news. While Terence was in surgery, I miscarried. It had been just two months. That was hard.

Wanting to Grow Up

The real on being married is about putting each other first. No one is above God, but each other are primary. Both must be supportive to each other. Encourage each other. Find time for each other. Often, I wanted the kids to be included. Terence wanted just us to spend time together. I had to listen. Listen to ensure that you are providing what the other desires and needs in the relationship.

My advice to couples is simple. Continue to date each other. Don't lose the relationship because of the title. You must be willing to be all in. It is a life of compromises including going along. Communication is critical. Share your feelings. Share your life. Be the real you. Whatever you start is what will need to continue. Our challenge was that Terence understood that he should just handle somethings himself. The truth is that the two should process together. Above all, allow each other to grow. We realize that we are not the same people we started with. You both must want success in the marriage.

Chapter 7: On Our Own

My daughter was 3 years old. We felt like it was really happening. What was it? We really had no words for it. We just knew it was happening. Maybe *IT* was the relationship. Terence and I were very serious in our relationship. Moving and establishing our own was his desire as well. I wanted for my children what I had growing up, a loving home that was the foundation for any and every accomplishment I could hope for. But I also didn't want to leave my mom. I knew I had to. I wanted more for Terence, me, and my daughter.

My mother and I were together when she left her first marriage. We started a new journey together. We discussed it before we left. It was going to be the two of us. We were a pair and support for one another. I felt like I was letting her down. She had a boyfriend at the time, but that didn't make it any easier for me. I was her youngest child and we built this apartment together. I was contributing to the household budget, but I also knew that she wanted what was best for me.

The time came for me to tell her that I was moving. At this point I had my first child in tow. We were running out of space. Terence and I had begun to talk about marriage.

"Terence and I are looking at getting our own apartment."
"Where are you thinking?"

"Toward Antioch because that is what we can afford."

"If that's something you want to do. That is fine. You have a baby and you and Terence are doing well. Is there something that happened?"

"No, mom. I just want to give you and your boyfriend your space."

"Well, don't do it because you feel you are in the way. Just know that you need to consider all the implications of bills and expenses. It is real out there."

We were looking for a place and found one quicker than anyone would have anticipated. I walked in to tell my mom and I could see that her emotions were mixed.

"I am going to miss you and the baby."

"Mom, we will be here. My babysitter still lives downstairs." And that was that. I moved out and Terence and I moved in together. As promised, I would come to pick up the baby from the babysitter and spend some time with my mother each time.

Financial Shock

Life up to that point had been relatively simple I thought as I jumped into the deep end of the pool that is being on my own. Up until the move to our first apartment, life was about working, affording, and doing. It truly was a financial shock to be out on our own. I would complain when I visited my mom. From renter's insurance, cleaning supplies, in addition to the light bills and rent. There are many things that you don't anticipate. "You can do it." That were my mom's words.

We have a closeness in our relationship that is the result of several shared experiences in addition to her being my mother. If I'm truthful, our relationship is also because of her personality. Her matter of fact, direct approach has always worked for me whether we agree or not. If she says I can do it, I can do it. I needed to hear it from her. Because she said so, I was okay. Even today, I hold things she has said in high regard because I see them come to pass. It can be one word, but simply because it came from her, I am at ease.

A Different World

My siblings, though they grew up in the same household as me, chose different paths. It is a lesson in patience and humility for me. The challenge is doing well when others are not coming along. But I have learned to count my success as mine and know that others count their success as theirs. What I think of as success is not always shared by others.

My challenge is the uncertainty about whether you are becoming distant because you are growing or becoming distant because they are content, and I am not. Sometimes I don't feel like I fit in. Some that we grew up with are still doing the things that Terence and I have given up becoming better parents. We decided to grow up. Others don't seem to have taken that route in life. We worked hard to get to a place where we could make different choices. We have built to the point where we have something to lose.

That is the lesson and the challenge. It is a situation of having something to lose. I feel like I have something to lose. I also feel the pressure of not wanting to be embarrassed through anything that Terence or my children are doing in the streets. My marriage must work. My children must succeed. It must prove all those people wrong who counted me out, who gave their faulty two cents, and who remained stuck when they could have chosen to get unstuck. It is not payback or revenge. It is paying forward. My desire is to show even through my own fears, questions, and hesitation that it can be done. The first person I am showing is ME. I'm taking the leap into the pool, swimming, and hoping others see that they can too.

And there is the truth of the stuck in their old way peanut gallery. I feel like sometimes they become my motivators. We continue despite the negative comments from the naysayers and haters. They get mad and say what they mean. They wish failure on us. They flaunt their carefree, nothing-to-lose lifestyles. We don't have the luxury to live like they do.

Youth and Spoils

We planned and looked forward. We didn't have any skills. We had to get a skill set. Terence didn't have a GED at the time. We both needed to go back to school. Giving birth, a decision to grow up, and the gift of time granted up some perspective. I wasn't going back to the insurance company after giving birth, but someone called me with a $0.50 raise. That convinced me to give that job more time.

My first child was about 2 years old when I thought about getting a new job and increasing our income to afford a place of our own. By the time she was 10, we were thinking about owning a house. I applied at Family and Children's services and got the job. I was making $10.50. I knew we could pay the mortgage making that amount. We had established credit by then. We were working toward owning a house. We built our credit from paying rent and qualified for a home loan. One of Terence's buddies suggested that he only needed an 8th grade education to work at metro. His friend talked to the manager and helped him get the job. And we were into the reality of home ownership.

In 2010, I was laid off from Family & Children's Services. I was there for 7 years before being laid off. Terence had 8 years in at his job as a custodian and was laid off at the same time. We had not been in our purchased home long and were fearful of losing it due to us both losing our jobs at the same time. We had a pre-teen and a toddler. I was just starting school and dealing with some serious emotional turmoil. It was June 30,2010.

Wanting Your Own

The proof of being a grown up is not in the marriage, the children, or the home ownership. I am convinced that it is in the ability to work through and overcome the hardest times in your life. Those times try you and the relationships you have with others. The proving of those relationships makes them stronger. The testing of your faith makes you stronger. I am stronger and certain of those that have my back. I am also certain about who I am doing this for.

It's me, and Terence, and my children. Then, salute to all the others that pushed, prompted, and propelled me forward. June 30, 2010 did not break me. In fact, I lost a great deal of fear during that trial. I applied to Behavioral Health Services in Metro Police as an admin assistant. I got my Associate degree. I applied and completed Tennessee State University. I finished my BSW and that allowed me to apply for promotion positions. Terence got another job that he enjoys. The lesson for me was not just about landing on my feet. It was about landing in my purpose. The lesson for you is not to simply survive but the thrive.

Section III: Beyond More

Chapter 8: Our Family

I was paranoid by the time we were pregnant with my second child. The pregnancy was another planned pregnancy. The pregnancy was stressful. I held a lot of fear that I would lose the baby. I was over the top. In our previous attempt, I had miscarried after two months. It was understandable for what had happened, but the fear was intense. Everything from that moment was different. We were in a good place.

Completing Our Family

We wanted another baby. I was careful about everything. My doctor told me I had to let up on seafood. I stressed about not wanting to overdo things so much so that I stressed myself out. We also moved while I was pregnant as we moved into our first purchased home. We moved in May. My second daughter was born in October.

Being married caused us to desire that adult family experience. It felt right for us to have another child. We talked about how great it felt to expand the family. Tiara, our first daughter, was 10 years old and was talking about having a sibling. By this time, my sister had her second child. Tiara saw her cousins with siblings. My daughter wanted someone to play with after school. She idealized the opportunity. We would shop for the baby. She helped me open the presents for the baby shower. She loved it. We were getting the room painted for the new baby. Toys, baby bed, a changing table, and clothing excited her. It didn't wear off until Tamia Yvonne began to be curious about her stuff. She will have head bands from her sister and more.

She would play in her shoes. She moved things from her dresser. It causes problems, but they are close. She watches her big sister put her make-up on, dress, and do things. She really looks up to her. Her name came from the singer and basketball wife, Tamia Hill.

I was a bit older when Tamia arrived. I would not say that I made major mistakes, but it was important to ensure that Tamia was getting from me what she needed as a mom. Tiara knew me as mother, but I feel that I could have spent more time with her intentionally. I did more with the family once the second child came along.

Tiara enjoys family days even at 20 years old. It takes me back to the projects when we were younger. It was the family together for games, meals, and events. I hold on to that as my children age. My goal is to hold on to that no matter how old they get.

I have thought about waking up together at Christmas even as they have families of their own. I want to provide the environment that is supportive of that reality. I would like for our traditions to continue and take precedence. I can hope. Her current boyfriend's family opens gifts on Christmas Eve, so that doesn't seem to be a problem.

Fear of Mothering

The fear came because my mom was the greatest help to me with my first. She was not in the same house for the second child. I had a hard time after Tiara physically. I had to go back to the doctor multiple times. I could not take care of Tiara for about a month after the birth. I felt absent to some extent. When Tiara would cry, my mom and her boyfriend at the time would take care of her like she was their baby. When she had a cold, my mother would tell me when I needed to take her to the doctor.

With Tamia, I called my mom a lot. It was not just the difference in their ages, it was that I felt that I needed to relearn how to take care of a baby. That first month is critical to your reality shift. You learn yourself as a mother. Learning the baby's sleep habits, feeding schedule, types of crying, and more. It is a bonding month as well. The knowledge of your baby from this first month provides a foundation for future questions and uncertainty.

I was not sure that I could be the mom I wanted to be. I had a definition of motherhood that included comfort and support. I was there to make sure that she felt safe, loved, and knowing my scent. I wanted her to trust and rely on me to be there. I felt like I could be that mother. I received that from my mother. I also created pressure to do it the right way, like the way my mom did it. My mom would do a lot of talking to Tiara. I wanted to be sure that I could do that. My mother's way was the right way that I needed to replicate.

Now, I don't feel there is a right way or a wrong way. You have to parent in a way that speaks to the mother in you. Of course, bad parenting exists. But that is when the child does not feel safe and loved. If you feel that you are a great mother, you children will let you know by how adventurous and outspoken they are. If they feel safe and loved, they are less hesitant and uncertain in their actions. Parents must make sure they make the time for their children. Providing is one thing, but communication is crucial to their development.

Resilience

When Terence and I sit down, we enjoy the now, but we are looking ahead. Tiara and Tamia are so different. We laugh about how they resemble people in our families. We joke about how they will engage with us when they become adults.

Tamia is on the cheerleading squad. Her tastes have changed from toys to foods to friends. Tiara continues to connect with us, but she also has her time with boyfriend, college, and other interests. We make sure that we take time for us, Terence and I. We plan our date nights. We talk about what is going on and about the future. The now may center on insurance or bills that we are contemplating. Future topics include ventures, business, and retirement. We maintain a strong foundation for enjoying each other's company. We get out and socialize with things that we both like to do.

We were high school sweethearts. We were tasked to grow up together. It is a unique challenge because interests change. I can't count on the same Terence that I knew 15 years ago or 10 years ago. Terence must know that Schlitta is changing. We have friends that married around the same time as us. They grew apart. We have discussed how it happens. If one person in the couple is not supportive of the growth and opportunity of the other, a wedge is built. Marriage, especially young marriage, is about allowing the spouse to be themselves. Enable them to enjoy who they are.

Beyond Wanting More: Accepting Growth

I feel blessed that Terence allows me to be me. He brags on me. He is proud of me. He celebrates me. If I bring an idea, he encourages me. When I'm involved, he asks with interest and support. I support him just the same. We always talk about finances and decision making. Money issues ruin many marriages. We share our purchases and expenses. It is important that I allow him to be a man and be himself.

The lesson for you must be about sharing and holding tightly to what matters, but also about letting go of those things that don't. Refuse the notion to hang on to something that is not working. But make sure you invest your all in those things that are important to you. Push past the fear of what you can't do, marshal your supports, and give your best. Whatever the outcome, grow.

Chapter 9: Post-Partum Depression

I felt different after I had my second child. It is hard to describe. I should have been happy. We were all enjoying the baby. I just wasn't quite myself. I felt like I could move through it. It was a relief. It was abnormal for me to have those feelings. I did not know why I was feeling like I was. My family was fine. I would cry. I would feel sad. It occurred to me that my hormones were everywhere. I considered that it was because I was older and having a baby, but I wasn't older.

My symptoms included not wanting to get out of bed. Prior to the birth, I was excited about the maternity leave. I was going to walk. I had a list of things I was going to do around the house. I am the type that normally wants to get out. I was laying there in the morning. Even on beautiful days, I could not muster the drive to do anything. I felt like I was being unfair to the baby. Terence went back to work before me. My older daughter was back in school. I would look at the baby and cry. I would get up to feed her and crawl right back into bed. I just knew that it wasn't me and I didn't want to feel that way. I didn't want to cry in the shower, forego food, and not know why. I was empty and drained.

I was always myself when around others and hide it well. I was the strong one, in everyone else's eyes so how dare I say I'm dealing with depression. My mother, father and sisters looked at me as the stronger one. No one knew but Terence. She cried a lot. Terence

helped with that. He put the effort into going to see about her because he knew that I was having trouble.

I finally went to see the Dr. The nurse came in first. I explained
to her what was going on and I was teary eyed. I had the baby and
was telling her my story. By the time the doctor came in, I was balling. He told me that his wife experienced the same thing. He told me
that it was normal. He went through the spiel about what happens
after a baby. I went to Dr. and took medication, but the meds were
not for me. He introduced it as a trial to see if it would help. He went
over the precautions and instructions for taking the medication.

I took the medication for about a week. It made me feel like I
wasn't myself. I added jittery and paranoid to the feelings I had orig-
inally. I would sit and feel like I was anxious. It was a different anxiety
from the feelings of before.

Mannequin

The event had been talked about. It was a women's conference
that we were doing at the church. She called it Women of Worth
WOW. Twice a month, the committee would meet. I was on the
committee. We would meet for about 2 hours.

I told Terence that I really needed to go to the conference, but I
was tired. I did not want to go. I was feeling down. Terence encouraged me. He reminded me of all the work I had put into the event. I
decided to go.

"This is what the Lord put on my heart. We look good, we feel
good. But, some of you are feeling like this underneath." Sticky notes
on the mannequin. You look like the mannequin, but underneath the

clothing, this is what you are feeling. It was me. It was what I was going through.

I started balling. No one knew about this but Terence. I had not even told my mom. At that moment, I felt like it was okay for me to release it. I remember her coming over and a couple of other ladies. They prayed for me.

When I left there, I felt good. First, I had told someone other than my husband. They weren't my family, but they were my church family. Second, they genuinely cared. They told about how they had felt like that before in their own lives. It helped me get through it.

If you share what you are going through, you can receive confirmation, encouragement, and empowerment. When you are sharing with someone who genuinely cares about you and they listen and understand, you cannot comprehend what that will do. You may smile and appear to be a strong person. You may be counted on to be the strong person. You may not feel that you can lean on others. That's how I felt. So, I held it. Once I shared, I was able to let it go. I felt like I had a weight on me. This is the first step in the healing process.

I want everyone to have someone that they can confide in. You want to discern who you are around. When you find that people are encouraging, speak to them. You may be tempted to second-guess your feelings and what you see. You may say to yourself, "They seem to be encouraging, but I don't know them like that." Go with your first mind and speak up. That will tell you who they are. You may find that you have the support to release the weight you have been carrying.

When I came home, Terence commented in the difference in me. The conference was really what I needed. I focused on staying encouraged. I was determined to speak life in those situations when I felt down, "Not today!"

Recovery

It should feel different by now. I feel like a lot of things that was positive for women. My grandmother's favorite verse was the 23rd Psalm. It became mind. I focused on that verse. I turned back to my roots of reading my bible and studying scripture, reading positive quotes, making sure I got some me time alone with candles burning. Faith and love got me through and realizing that I was loved very much. I would say the depression lasted about a year.

The 23rd Psalm was a great help in my senior year. That experience rushed back to me in waves. I remembered how the verse got me through. I felt that I needed to get back to it. Use what works for you. Find that sustainable option. Use it to get past this challenging moment. Use it to heal and get healthy. The goal is what works. Often, people are mad at God or have other strong emotions about what may have been important to them at the time. It may not be a Bible verse or any expression of God. It could be talking and processing. The comfort can come from a support group. Expressing emotions is a common tool for getting through. Expression could be through art, recreation, or something else. Therapy is another option.

I grew up in a house where going to therapy was allowing people to get in your business. A lot of Black households I know are like mine was. I am open to therapy. Terence and I received counseling before we were married. I encouraged my daughter to utilize my EAP benefits when she graduated from high school. She had some adjustment questions. She never went, but knowing that she could, knowing that she could attend with me or by herself. I told her what it was about. She thought it was all about being prescribed medication. My mother attended counseling after the death of my stepfather. She benefitted from it.

Beyond Wanting More: Accepting Help

I am grateful that I found the opportunity to share with my church family. Their genuineness connected me. If I could change what happened, I would have talked to more than just my husband sooner. I would definitely have confided in my mother. You must admit to yourself that you are human like everyone else. You don't always have to be the strong person. My experience opened my eyes to the fact that it could happen to anyone. It happened to me.

Chapter 10: The Future Beyond Wanting More

I want to enjoy life. At 42 years old, I continue to learn. I have learned more about myself. My future feels like time for resilience. It looks like coping during challenging times is the order of the day. Building resilience to face life's challenges is critical. If you can change your situation, change it. If you can't change it, wait patiently for the opportunity to come.

Women and Girls

Find that healing place. Each day we learn something about ourselves. It begins with loving yourself, knowing who you are, moving in faith not fear.

Loving Yourself. Make sure that you have time for you. Cherish alone time. Even if it is getting a manicure or pedicure, do it. I am working up the courage to go out of town or out of the country by myself. Whether I do or not, discover whether that's something you want to do or not. It may not be school or career. It doesn't have to be travel or experience. The goal is to make sure it is your truth. Revolve it around your schedule and your planning. It will feel strange at first. You may have people who are uncomfortable with it. But this self-care is vital.

Knowing You. Sometimes, we focus and define ourselves through family. We lose ourselves. Or, more directly, we give ourselves away. We must, instead, discover more about ourselves. Our plans can't revolve around our children. Our womanhood can revolve around our husbands. Take time to reflect on what you want to accomplish. You may have been doing the same routine for years. As the family grows, the children get older, your relationships and network become stronger and more diverse. You are in a space of finding yourself. Find the you that is the grown up at this time in your life.

Faith and Not Fear. Follow your dreams. It is as simple as doing something different for yourself. You can. I don't know where the disconnect is for some. I want to ask what they are thinking. I want to encourage them to think a different way. I want them to get another message from someone close.

Being the Bigger Person

More people come from the same place I have come from. We didn't grow up with a lot of resources. Get out and engage with people that are different from you. I never knew I was poor until I got out of the neighborhood. For some, this results in covetousness or wanting what others have. But that's incomplete. Don't just have what they have. Go beyond doing what they do. Become the person you want to be. If you can become that person, you will never fear losing what you accomplish. You continue to learn in those networks. Someone knows what you need to know. That socializing expands your resources of information. That information expansion translates into ability.

I can use my education to inspire people to work through their fears. They have fears that I had. I feel like it would take someone bigger than me to help them. But I can be that bigger person by continuing my development and sharing my journey. The first step is this book.

No More Listen and Go Home

Since I started this book, I realized that fear was the thing that kept me from a lot of things. I wanted more, but I was fearful of what it was. I am awakening to my calling and recognizing the difference between an okay life and the life I'm called to live.

You must figure out what the calling is and go after it. I saw a quote about fear. "Fear can be present. It doesn't have to rule." I receive that. I tell my children to push past fear. I tell them to live to their full potential. I realize that I have allowed fear to slow me down. Buying a house, starting a family, getting married, all of these potentially hold fear. I am now more comfortable moving forward instead of procrastinating.

Better You. Discovering yourself. As women, we don't stop and think about our purpose, calling, and what God is telling us in any moment. Getting involved, relying on scripture can help you with a sense of self-worth, knowing who you are, building a relationship with Christ, and establishing your calling in the church. I had to discover where I fit in with the ministry.

Purpose. You can accept that there is learning available to you. Women are nurturers. We pour into others and forget that we need to be filled. When you return to the scripture and read, you recognize confirmation for your purpose. We often second guess ourselves before we return it to god even through scripture. Meditation helps with this. Meditation is quiet time to listen and focus on what god is saying to you. You can hear the voice of god speaking, leading you to what you should focus on next.

Connection. You don't have to do this by yourself. I was one of those people. I did not want to be judge. I thought that no one was experiencing life like I was. I didn't think anyone would understand. I found out that the things that were happening to me were experiences that other women shared.

It was hard for me to figure out how to articulate the challenge. I didn't know if I could say it in a way that would connect and get my point across. I desperately wanted to be understood, which made me hesitate not wanting to be misunderstood. I want women to know that you must try. You will find like I did that other women are ready to nurture you.

It's like when you are sitting in a classroom not wanting to ask a question. But others may want to ask the question as well. Women are thankful that you share because they feel that they can share. Their story finds voice in your story. They feel that maybe they can share. Maybe they have someone they can confide in because you shared.

Build With. There are more things that you can get help with than things you want to keep private and separate from others. You don't want people to be bossy, critical, or judgmental. But you can use support, counsel, and encouragement. Don't get the two confused. When you connect with other women, the possibilities are endless. It may begin with a relationship. You gain meaningful connection with someone who sees the world closer to your view than a man does. Relationship may develop into friendship. You gain a partner for experiences and create shared stories. Friendship supports a platform for your dreams and aspirations. Your enjoyment increases as your bond strengthens. The next level is family. At that point, the bond is different and unbreakable. You share within that circle without judgment. You share all of you openly including the good, bad, ugly, mistakes, successes, and failures.